What Was the Boston Tea Party?

by Kathleen Krull

illustrated by Lauren Mortimer

Penguin Workshop
An Imprint of Penguin Random House

To all my teacher friends—KK

PENGUIN WORKSHOP
Penguin Young Readers Group
An Imprint of Penguin Random House LLC

Library of Congress Control Number: 2012027570

ISBN 9780448462882

15

Contents

What Was the Boston Tea Party?

Boston, the night of December 16, 1773

What a strange tea party. It took place in near darkness and in almost total silence. It lasted for about three hours. There were no women there, just men, many in their teens. It was dangerous to be a guest at this tea party. Anyone caught would be arrested and face serious punishment. So most came in disguise.

Did the guests drink tea? No. Not a single sip. They boarded three ships in Boston Harbor and hoisted 342 chests of tea overboard. Fortunately only a couple of people were hurt, one who was caught stealing tea and beaten up, and another who was injured when a heavy tea chest fell on him.

So it was not really a party at all. Rather, the
Boston Tea Party was one of the most powerful

protests ever, rocking the world and in time leading to the birth of a whole new country.

CHAPTER 1
Why Taxes? Why Tea?

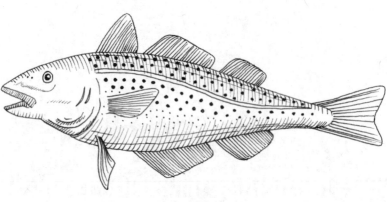

Codfish

In the 1700s, Boston reeked of horse manure and garbage, unless fresh, salty air from the harbor breezed through. Food odors blended in—clam chowder, lots of fresh codfish, stewed pumpkin, bread, whatever the neighbor was cooking. Everyone lived jammed together on crooked streets that narrowed down toward the waterfront.

Something else was in the air—rebellion. Boston was getting known as the city most likely to question authority. Whose authority? The king of England, George III. The king was determined to punish the colonies for any sign of rebellion, and American colonies only thought of him as a tyrant.

King George III

Mohawk Indians

By 1765, the people of the thirteen colonies in America were puffed with pride. They were thriving an ocean away from Great Britain. They'd cleared forests, farmed the land, built homes. There were towns and cities. Colonists now outnumbered the original inhabitants, the American Indians, by twenty to one.

The Thirteen Colonies

Each colony acted almost like a separate country. And even though the colonies belonged to England, they made their own local laws. In Virginia there was a group called the House of Burgesses. Pennsylvania had its General Assembly. And in Massachusetts, there was a House of Representatives.

Ben the Poet

Benjamin Franklin

This is part of a funny poem that shows how many of the colonists felt about Great Britain. They believed the king of England was still treating them like little children who couldn't take care of themselves. Benjamin Franklin wrote the poem. He is known as one of the Founding Fathers of the United States. He helped write the Declaration of Independence and the United States Constitution.

We have an old mother that peevish is grown,

She snubs us like children that scarce walk alone;

She forgets we're grown up and have sense of our own,

Which nobody can deny, deny, which nobody can deny.

Boston, Massachusetts, was the richest
shipping center in America, buzzing with energy.

Half of Boston's population of sixteen thousand was under sixteen.

Everyone, even children, worked hard. Boston had three thousand houses of wood and brick, some five hundred shops, and eleven churches—not to mention one hundred taverns.

Old North Church

Along the shoreline were wharves and shipyards to service all the cargo ships that sailed in and out of the harbor.

THE
Boston-
AND
COUNTRY
Gazette,
JOURNAL

MONDAY, January 15 1770

Boston also boasted great newspapers and a high percentage of people who could read.

While women raised huge families, men made their livings keeping shops, crafting fine goods such as silver tea sets, working on ships, or fishing, among other trades. Because the recent French and Indian War had killed many men, women outnumbered them.

The war had lasted seven rough years. Great Britain, with the help of the colonists, had won. The king of England now ruled over even more land in North America.

But the war had been very costly. Britain had nearly emptied its treasury and owed what would amount to billions of dollars in today's money. And Parliament insisted on being paid back by America.

When did they want the money?

Immediately!

Parliament, the governing body which made laws in Great Britain, had no members from the colonies.

Then in 1765, Parliament imposed the Stamp Act on America. This was an attempt to collect money from the Americans.

Parliament of Great Britain

Suddenly paper items—newspapers, legal documents, playing cards—had to have an official stamp, paid for with a tax.

A tax? No one likes paying taxes—money that goes to the government to pay for the services it provides its citizens. Up until now, Americans had paid no direct taxes, and they liked it that way. It was one reason why the colonies had been prospering. The stamp tax was the first major tax on the colonies and the first on American-made items. It affected almost everyone.

Colonists did not approve. They didn't have any representation or say in what the British government decided. It wasn't fair that Parliament had the power to tax them.

In Boston, the Stamp Act was like a bomb. There were riots. Marchers in the streets chanted, "Liberty, property, and *no stamps*!" Mobs threw stamped documents on bonfires and hurled rocks

and bricks at British officials. They nearly destroyed Thomas Hutchinson's grand house. He was the unpopular British governor of Massachusetts.

Hutchinson fled to Fort William, an island

fortress in Boston Harbor. At first, he tried to be reasonable with the rebels. He understood that people like to complain about what their government is doing to them. As he put it, "There is nothing so easy as to persuade people that they are badly governed . . . this is one of the weaknesses

Thomas Hutchinson

of human nature." But when Hutchinson revealed himself to be firmly in favor of the British law, he became the most hated man in Boston. After the Tea Party, he lost his job and went back to England. He was replaced by Thomas Gage, a strong general.

Boston was not alone in protesting. It was, in fact, the first time many in the colonies all felt the same way: The Stamp Act had to go.

Shocked by the violence, the British Parliament ended the Stamp Act the following year.

There was serious partying in Boston the night people found out. The richest man in town, John Hancock, set off flashy fireworks in front of his house. And he supplied fine wine for the crowd.

John Hancock

So was Parliament done with taxing the colonists? No. The Townshend Acts came in 1767. Now goods brought into America were taxed—paint, paper, lead, glass, and the latest colonial fad: tea.

Some colonists were getting angrier by the minute.

CHAPTER 2
Children Die in Boston

Samuel Adams of Boston was one angry guy. He was among the first to urge Americans to unite and break away from England. To the British he was "the most dangerous man in Massachusetts."

Adams's father had once owned the largest brewery in Boston, turning barley into beer. But he lost all his money.

Samuel Adams

Samuel studied at Harvard College. That was where his anger toward Britain began. Back then he kept his feelings to himself. Calling for the end

Harvard College

of British rule was treason. Treason was a crime punishable by death.

After college, Samuel failed at just about everything he tried. He spent his evenings in taverns where men talked about the events of the day. They also enjoyed smoking "till you cannot see from one end . . . to the other," according to his cousin John Adams.

Samuel Adams

Samuel Adams said he hated money, and he was certainly bad at making it. Seedy looking in a ragged red jacket and cheap gray wig, he appeared much older than he was. He had a tremor in his head and hands that got worse when he was upset. But his cousin John praised his "most thorough understanding of liberty [and] good character."

He is not among the most famous of the Founding Fathers, the men who first fought to make the colonies free of England and start a new country. After the colonies became the United States of America in 1776, Samuel Adams remained active in politics. He was a three-and-a-half-term governor of Massachusetts and died in 1803.

Many people confuse him with his much more famous cousins (John and John Quincy, the second and sixth presidents). If his name is known today, it is mainly because of a certain beer. The Boston Beer Company started manufacturing Samuel Adams beers in 1985. Not only did Adams not like to drink, but the portrait on the brand's label isn't even of him. It's of Paul Revere.

Samuel Adams blitzed newspapers with furious letters about Britain. He penned thousands of them. Sometimes he answered his own letters himself, using fake names, to make it seem as if all Boston was seething with anger.

It wasn't just the taxes that Bostonians like Samuel Adams resented. They suspected the king wanted to squash their power to govern themselves. They saw something evil at work, a plot brewing to take away their freedom. Samuel's followers were first called "Adams's Mohawks" for wearing Indian blankets to show their desire to live freely and simply.

According to the Massachusetts Charter, men who owned property could elect people to manage local issues. And they could hold town meetings to decide things like where to build roads, to set budgets, and to address any other matter affecting the welfare of the town. Power was local, not with a Parliament three thousand miles away.

After the Stamp Act, Boston workers and tradesmen founded the Sons of Liberty. It was a secret society of rebels who protested the stamp tax. It soon spread elsewhere. In Boston, members often met at the Liberty Tree, a one-hundred-year-old elm. Occasionally they hung a British tax collector from the tree—not a real man but a dummy.

Sometimes they punished tax collectors by tarring and feathering them. A mob would cover a man in hot tar, then roll him in bird feathers, sometimes beating him up. It wasn't fatal, but reports of it alarmed the British, who labeled the rebels "cannibals."

Other protests included boycotts of goods from Britain, such as clothes and tea. (A boycott means refusing to buy a certain thing or shop at

a certain store in order to express disapproval.)
Young girls were encouraged to take up spinning
and make their own clothes instead of buying

cloth from England. Young boys wrecked shops
where British goods were still sold. Sometimes
they smeared "night soil" (a term for human
excrement) on the walls of those shops.

The king had to put a stop to all this trouble.
In 1768 he sent troops to Boston, eventually

numbering four thousand soldiers. Dressed in bright red coats, the troops were to patrol the streets, put down protests, and protect loyalists.

Loyalists were the colonists who were on King George's side. It was the first time troops had been sent to police Americans, not to protect them.

The situation got worse. Children and teenagers often confronted the soldiers. They would hurl insults, plus snowballs, oysters, rotten eggs, and rocks.

In this tense atmosphere, a clash was sure to come.

One day, in a skirmish between loyalists and rebels, a loyalist fired shots. A nineteen-year-old was wounded and an eleven-year-old boy was killed.

The boy, Christopher Seider, was considered a hero who died for his country's cause. And his funeral was the largest ever held in America up to that time.

A couple of weeks later, on March 5, 1770, a crowd of colonists was insulting some British officers.

Nobody in the crowd was armed, but a
jumpy soldier fired his gun.

The first to die was Crispus Attucks, once a runaway slave, now a sailor. Four more were killed, including two seventeen-year-old boys.

A witness wept "to see the blood of our fellow citizens flowing down the gutters like water." Twelve thousand people showed up for the funerals.

The event on March 5 became known as the Boston Massacre. A massacre is the murder of a group of unresisting people. That is not exactly what happened in Boston. Nevertheless, in the coming years, Samuel Adams would

Crispus Attucks

remind Bostonians, "Remember the bloody Massacre!"

British officials remained at Fort William on Castle Island two miles away from Boston. It was a fortress of thick stone with lots of cannons.

Fort William

How did the British government react to all this? Seeking peace, Parliament repealed (or did

away with) all the taxes in the Townshend Acts—
all except for the small tax on tea. The British
government was showing that it was reasonable.
But it was also showing that it was still the boss
of America.

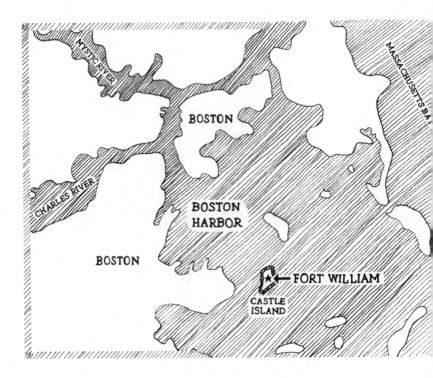

Some women formed their own rebel groups.
One group called themselves the Daughters of

Liberty. Some tried to break their tea habit once the tax went into effect. They made their own tea, from sage or raspberry leaves, and called it "Liberty Tea." Colonists could also avoid the tax by illegally smuggling in tea from Holland, unloading it from ships at night.

Samuel Adams and the Sons of Liberty were drawing more and more people in Boston—men, women, and children—to their side.

Then, in May 1773, Parliament passed an entire act just about tea—the Tea Act. Was Britain *trying* to rub it in?

Tea

Tea mattered to the colonists. They rarely drank fresh water because they believed it would make them sick. They washed down meals with rum, ale, wine, beer, and, increasingly, tea. They brewed the tea leaves, which came from China and India, in boiling water. (People believed, correctly, that boiling killed off any germs in the water.)

At first tea was a luxury item, just for rich people. But eventually almost anyone in the colonies could afford it. By the 1760s Americans were drinking a lot of tea. People loved brewing it and serving it  in pretty teapots for company. The richest had tea sets made of silver.

CHAPTER 3
At the Green Dragon Tavern

Green Dragon Tavern

No one worked harder to get rid of the tea tax than Samuel Adams—and he didn't even like the taste of tea. He met with other men in taverns like the Green Dragon and, as the meetings got larger, at Faneuil Hall.

There was his plump younger cousin (and

Faneuil Hall

future president) John Adams. John was a rising

young lawyer. He ranted that the Stamp Act would "drain the country of its cash, strip multitudes of all their property, and reduce [people] to absolute beggary."

John Adams

John Hancock was very different from the Adams cousins. He wore suits of red velvet and lived in a mansion on Beacon Hill. He, too, was a rebel, yet he worried about protecting his property from violent mobs. He thought Samuel Adams was a political genius and figured Adams had enough influence with the mobs to keep Hancock's property safe. He also began funding the Sons of Liberty. A strong speaker, Hancock was popular with everyone and very generous to the poor. John Hancock went on to become the first American governor of Massachusetts

Hancock's mansion on Beacon Hill

in 1780 and became more beloved than ever.

Paul Revere was a faithful friend to the Sons of Liberty—an expert silversmith whose work was in demand. If you wanted to pour your tea from a beautiful silver teapot, Paul Revere was the man to see. Also, his skill as a horseman made him a

Paul Revere

A street view of colonial Boston that includes the old statehouse

Created by Benjamin Franklin, this was the first political cartoon in American history. Its message means the colonies would only survive if united.

Houses of Parliament, London

Teapot made by Paul Revere

*Paul Revere. Maker: Paul Revere, Jr., 1734–1818. Teapot. 1796. Silver, Overall: 6 1/16 x 11 5/8 in. (15.4 x 29.5 cm); 21 oz. 10 dwt. (668.7 g).
Base: 5 11/16 x 3 3/4 in. (14.4 x 9.5 cm). Bequest of Alphonso T. Clearwater, 1933. (33.120.543). Made in: America, Northeast, Massachusetts,
Boston. The Metropolitan Museum of Art, New York, NY, USA

Portrait of King George III

A tax stamp

British officer with soldiers

Fires in reaction to the Stamp Act

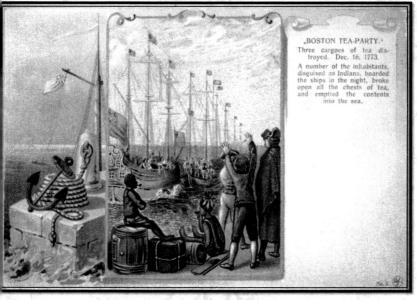

What the Boston Tea Party might have looked like

George Washington, shown
here as a Virginian colonel

Governor Hutchinson
as a young man

John Hancock

Paul Revere

A New Method of MACARONY MAKING, as practifed at BOSTON.

A tarred and feathered British customs officer

Boston Harbor with two ships at anchor, British soldiers, and men working

Men pulling down a statue of King George III in New York.

THE DESTRUCTION OF TEA AT BOSTON HARBOR.

Another depiction of what the Tea Party may have looked like

The Green Dragon.

The Green
Dragon Tavern

This illustration appeared in a book published one hundred years after
the Boston Tea Party.

Paul Revere's engraving of the Boston Massacre

No. 779.

THE Boston- Gazette,

AND COUNTRY JOURNAL.

Containing the freshest Advices, Foreign and Domestic.

MONDAY, March 12, 1770.

Like a scurvy politician seem,
To see the things thou dost not.
  SHAKESPEARE.

A Writer, in the Boston Chronicle, has not only been charged, in direct terms, but *proved*, guilty of *impertinence,absurdity, sophistry* & *falsehood*. That, all this has been done, with fair argument and good manners, the BOSTONIAN ought, with blushes, to concede. But should that gentleman think such a concession too great a facrifice to truth and justice, it is then hoped, that his future publications, the' *unanswer'd*, will meet little attention, and less credit. For, furely, when a writer, after fuch *charges* and fuch *proofs*, continues to *vapour* and *froth*, in futile harms and indeterminate expreffions, devoid of reafon or excufe, he cannot rationally hope even the countenance of a *party*.

Such a profound ignorance of the laws and conftitution of our government is difplayed in the laft pro'ufion, figned a BOSTONIAN, that it is very difficult to refrain, from expreffions of contempt ; fuch trifling evafion and defpicable argument are below ferious confutation.

To acknowledge *allegiance* to the King, and deny obedience to the *laws* of Great-Britain, the BOSTONIAN fays would be prepofterous." As well might he afert, that an acknowledgement of *duty* to a *natural* parent was incompatible with an abfolute denial of obedience to his *unnatural* demands. But the weaknefs of what is, here, called, "prepofterous", muft be peculiarly evident to thofe,who are acquainted with the fpirit of our laws : And if fome fay true, our B OSTONIAN ought to be much *afhamed* of his defects, in handling this fubject.

I would caufe to treat every publick writer with politenefs, but when palpable lies are aferted, for truth, in the face of all mankind, it is difficult to abftain from an appearance of incivility. —The BOSTONIAN is called upon to offer the *leaft* fhadow of evidence, that——'the Independant would convert *every* province or ifland, *however infignificant* fome of them may be, into *feparate* and *diftinct* ftates :"—

It would require little lefs than a fpirit of divination to find out, what reafon or propriety there was in the flated fuppofition, about " the people of Main". The BOSTONIAN furely expofes himfelf to very juft ridicule ! Matters of greater importance, than viewing the defects and deformities of the BOSTONIAN, demand our inftant attention. I therefore, clofe with the very applicable fentiments of an author, whofe ftrength and life were fpent in the fervice of his GOD and his country.

" Few words, well confidered ; few and eafy things, now feafonably done ; will fave us. But if the people be fo affected,as to proftitute religion and liberty, to the vain and groundlefs apprehenfion, that nothing, but a lucrative trade can make them happy ; and if trade be grown fo craving and importunate that the profufion of men, that nothing can fupport it, but the luxurious expences of the people fhould generally facrifice themfelves to frugality, it might prove a dangerous matter, left tradefmen fhould mutiny, for want of trading ; and that, therefore, we muft forego and fet to fale, religion, liberty, honour, fafety, all concernment divine or human, to keep up trading ; if, laftly, after all this light among us, the fame reafon fhall pafs for current to fix our necks under illegal impofitions, as was made ufe of, by the Jews, to,return back to Egypt, becaufe they foolifhly imagined, that they would then live in more plenty and profperity ; our condition is not found but rotten, both in religion and all civil prudence ; and we fhall then be brought to thofe calamities, which attend always and unavoidably on luxury, that is to fay, all national judgments under foreign and domeftic flavery.

Thus, with hazard, I have ventured, what I thought my duty, to fpeak in feafon, and to forewarn my country in time. Many circumftances and particulars I could have added ; but a few

---

main matters, now put fpeedily into execution, will fuffice to recover us frombondage, and fet all right.— Whas I have faid, is the language of the GOOD OLD CAUSE : If itfeem ftrange to any, it will not feem more ftrangel hope, than convincing to backfliders. Thus much I fhould perhaps have faid, tho' fure I fhould have fpoken, only, to trees and ftones, and had more to ery to, but with the prophet ; *O earth, earth, earth* ! But, I truft, I fhall have fpoken perfuafion to abundance of fenfible and ingenuous men ; to fome,perhaps, whom GOD may raife of thefetones, to bcome children of liberty ; and may enable and unite in noble refolution to give a full ftay to the ruinous proceedings of tyranny and rapine."

AN INDEPNDANT.

At a Meeting of the Freeholders and other Inhabitants of the Town of Roxbury, legally affembled, on Monday the 5th Day of March, 1770, the Inhabitants taking into Confideration a Claufe in the Warrant for calling faid Meeting, viz. And to know the Minds of the Town Whether they will do any Thing to ftrengthen the Hands of the Merchants in their Non-Importation Agreement :

VOTED,

THAT Capt. William Hefh, Col. Jofeph Williams, Mr. Eleazer Weld, Capt. Jofeph Mayo, and Doctor Thomas Williams, be a Committee to take this Matter into Confideration, and report to the Town what they fhall think proper to be done thereon.

The Meeting was then adjourn'd to the 8th Inftant, Two o'Clock Afternoon ; at which Time the Inhabitants being again affembled, the Committee made the following Report, viz.

WHEREAS the Merchants and Traders of the Town of Bofton, and almoft all the Maritime Towns on the Continent, from a Principle truly noble and generous, and to the facrificing of their own private Interefts, have entred into an Agreement not to import Britifh Goods (a few neceffary Articles excepted) until the Act of Parliament impofing certain Duties on Tea, Glafs, Paper, Painters Colours, Oyl, &c. for the exprefs Purpofe of raifing a Revenue in America, be repealed ; which Agreement, if ftrictly adhered to, will not fail to produce the moft falutary Effects. Therefore,

VOTED, That the Inhabitants of this Town do highly applaud the Conduct and Refolution of faid Merchants and Traders : And we do take this Opportunity to exprefs our warmeft Gratitude to faid Merchants, for the fpirited Meafures which they have taken. And we do hereby declare,that we will, to the utmoft of our power, and aid affift faid Merchants, in every conftitutional Way, to render faid Agreement effectual.

VOTED, That we do with the utmoft Abhorrence and Deteftation, view the little, mean and fordid Conduct of a few Traders in this Province, who have and ftill do import Britifh Goods contrary to faid Agreement, and have thereby difcovered that they are governed by a felfifh Spirit,and are regardlefs of, and deaf to, the Miferies and Calamities which threaten this people.

VOTED, That whereas *John Bernard, James Mc Maffers, Patrick McMaffers, John Mein,Nathaniel Rogers, William Jackfon, Theophilus Lillie, John Taylor,* and *Ann & Elizabeth Cummings,* all of Bofton ; *Ifrael Williams* Efq; & Son of Hatfield ; & *Henry Barnes* of Marlboro', are of this Number ; and do import contrary to faid Agreement : We do hereby declare, that we will not buy the leaft Article of any of faid perfons ourfelves, or fuffer any acting for or under us, to buy of them ; neither will we buy of thofe that fhall buy or exchange any articles of Goods with them.

VOTED, That to the End the Generations which are yet unborn, may know who they were that laughed at the Diftreffes and Calamities of this people ; and inftead of ftriving to fave their Country when in imminent Danger, did ftrive to render ineffectual a virtuous and commendable Plan ; the Names of thefe Importers fhall be annually read at March Meeting.

VOTED, That we will not make ufe of any Foreign Teas inour feveral Families, until the Revenue Afare repealed (Cafe of Sicknefs excepted.)

VOTED, That a Committee of Infpection be chofen, to make Enquiry from Time to Time,how far thefe Votes are complied with.

VOTED, That a Copy of thefe Votes be tranfmitted to the Committee of Infpection in the Town of Bofton.

At a Meeting of the Inhabitants of the Town of Littleton, in the County of Middlefex, on Monday March 5th, 1770, a Committee was chofen the March 5th, 1770, who after retiring a fhort Time into a private Room, returned, and reported the following, which was unanimoufly Voted.

THE grievous Impofitions the Inhabitants of the Britifh Colonies have long fuffered from their Mother Country, ftrongly claim their Attention in every legal Method for their Removal.

WE efteem the Meafure already propofed, viz. the withdrawing our Trade fromEngland, both œconomical and effectual.

WE do therefore, Vote,

1. THAT we will not (knowingly) directly or indirectly, purchafe any Goods which now are or hereafter may be imported contrary to the Agreement of theMerchants of the Town of Bofton.

2. That if any Inhabitant of the Town of Littleton, fhall be known to purchafe any one Article of any Importer of Goods contrary to the before-mentioned Agreement, or of any one who fhall buy of any fuch Importer, he fhall fuffer our high Difpleafure and Contempt.

3. That a Committee be chofen to infpect the Conduct of all Buyers and Sellers of Goods in this Town, and report the Names of all (if any fuch there fhould be) who fhall violate the true Spirit and Intention of the above-mentioned Votes and Refolutions.

4. That we will not drink or purchafe any foreign Tea, howfoever Imported, until a general Importation of Britifh Goods fhall take Place.

THE Inhabitants of the Town of *Adon*, at their annual Town Meeting on the firft Monday of March, 1770, taking into Confideration the diftreffed circumftances, that this Province and all North-America are involv'd in, by reafon of the acts of Parliament impofing Duties and Taxes, upon the Inhabitants of North-America, for the fole purpofe to raife a Revenue, and when the Royal Ear feems to be ftopt againft all our humble Prayers, and Petitions, for redrefs of Grievances, that this Land is involv'd in, and confidering the falutary Meafures that the Body of Merchants and Traders in this Province have come into, in order for the redrefs of the many troubles that we are involv'd in, and to fupport and maintain our Charter Rights, and Privileges, and to prevent our total Ruin and Deftruction : Making all thefe things into feriousConfideration, came into the following Votes.

VOTED, That we will ufe our utmoft Endeavours to encourage and fupport the Body of Merchants and Traders, in their falutary Endeavours to retrieve this Province out of its prefent Diftrefs, to whom this Town vote their Thanks for the conftitutional and fpiritedMeafures purfued by them for the good of this Province.

Voted, That from this Time, we will have no commercial, or focial connection, with thofe, who at this Time do refufe to contribute to the relief of this abufed Country, efpecially, thofe that import Britifh Goods, contrary to the Agreement of the Body of Merchants in Bofton, or elfewhere, that we will not afford them ourCuftom, but treat them with the utmoft Neglect, and all thofe who countenance them.

VOTED, That we will ufe our utmoft Endeavours, to prevent the Confumption of all foreign Superfluities, and that we will ufe our utmoft Endeavours, to promote and encourage our own Manufactures.

VOTED, That the Town Clerk tranfmit a Copy of thefe Votes of the Town, to the Committee of Merchants of Infpection at Bofton.

A true Copy Attefted,
FRANCIS FAULKNER, *Town Clerk.*

The Boston Gazette, and Country Journal, March 12, 1770, on the Boston Tea Party

[January, 1770]

WILLIAM JACKSON,

an *IMPORTER*; at the

BRAZEN HEAD,

North Side of the TOWN-HOUSE,

and *Opposite the Town-Pump, in*

Corn-hill, BOSTON.

It is defired that the Sons and
DAUGHTERS of *LIBERTY,*
would not buy any one thing of
him, for in fo doing they will bring
Difgrace upon *themfelves,* and their
Pofterity, for *ever* and *ever,* AMEN.

Handbill calling for the Sons and Daughters of Liberty to
boycott imported goods

Benjamin Franklin

JOHN ADAMS.

John Adams

Samuel Adams

Benjamin Franklin,
the printer

This shows the surrender of Cornwallis but is full of errors. For instance, Cornwallis was not actually there.

The signing of the Declaration of Independence

legendary messenger for the rebels.

Every day, the Sons of Liberty had more to rant about, even though the Tea Act of 1773, which kept the tax, did have one benefit for Americans. It cut the price of tea in half.

How did that happen?

Britain wanted to help out a powerful British company called the East India Company. It sold, among other things, tea from India and China. The company was struggling. Its warehouses held eighteen million pounds of unsold tea. So Parliament said that colonists *had* to buy tea from the East India Company. In return, they would get it at a cheap price.

Boston was abuzz. They resented the tea tax. *And* they resented being told where to buy their tea. (They'd been able to smuggle it from Holland before.)

Who knew? Maybe soon the British would start demanding that colonists buy other things—

like tools or clothes—only from England. That just wasn't fair.

In October, newspapers reported that ships from England bearing tea were sailing straight for Boston Harbor. Rebels said this was "a violent attack upon the liberties of America." Samuel Adams called it "more to be dreaded than plague." It wasn't about tea, but about freedom.

The first ship arrived on November 28, and soon two more ships were in the harbor at Griffin's Wharf. The names of the ships were the *Dartmouth*, the *Eleanor*, and the *Beaver*.

Their combined cargo was 342 heavy chests packed with tea. A fourth ship, holding fifty-eight

chests of tea, foundered off Cape Cod.

The rebels and their supporters were dead set against accepting the tea. They demanded that the ships turn right around and sail back to England. The tea would not be unloaded.

But the ships refused to go. By law, they couldn't leave without dropping off their cargo first. So armed colonists made sure no chests of tea were taken off the ships and put on the wharf. Every half hour they'd call "All is well" to each other.

Boston was under mounting pressure. *Something* had to happen to this tea within twenty days, before midnight on the night of December 16. Otherwise British officials could seize it, start selling it, and charge the hated tax.

Other cities now were egging on Boston to step up and take action. Abigail Adams, the wife of John Adams, said, "The flame is kindled and like lightning it catches from soul to soul."

On November 29, notices went up all over Boston: "Friends! Brethren! Countrymen! That

Abigail Adams

worst of plagues, the detestable tea . . . is now arrived," the notices read, urging people to act now.

Boston had been holding public meetings protesting British rule. These gatherings were open to anyone, not just elected officials, not just the rich. The first meeting about the tea was so big—between five thousand and seven thousand people—that it had to be held in the Old South Meeting House. It was the largest building in town. In the unheated hall, amid the smell of

Old South Meeting House

unwashed bodies, people sat on hard wooden benches and stamped their feet to keep warm.

Governor Hutchinson sent a message ordering that one such meeting be shut down. Samuel Adams thought Hutchinson had some nerve. He retorted, "He? He? Is he that shadow of a man, scarce able to support his withered carcass or his hoary head! Is he a representation of *majesty*?"

The group refused to disband. Adams wanted the tea to be shipped back to England, the taxes unpaid. One person shouted that it should be thrown overboard. The Sons of Liberty leaders pretended to ignore the outburst. They wanted it to be on record that they were for preserving the tea, not destroying it. But that was just what they were saying in public. At top secret meetings, Adams and other leaders were planning to do exactly what the man had shouted. Dump the tea.

The final public meeting about the tea took place on the chilly, drizzly morning of

December 16, 1773. One last message was sent to Governor Hutchinson. Would he give the go-ahead for the ships—and the tea—to leave the harbor?

Hutchinson's answer was no.

Shouts echoed throughout the hall. Hancock's voice was heard saying, "Let every man do what is right in his own eyes."

Adams abruptly ended the meeting, calling, "This meeting can do nothing more to save the country." His words seemed to be a prearranged signal.

There was a loud whistle, and someone said, "Boston Harbor a teapot tonight!"

CHAPTER 4
Party Time

It was around six o'clock in the evening. About fifty men, some crudely dressed as American Indians, appeared at the back of the Old South Meeting House.

Two by two they began marching to Griffin's Wharf. Other men and boys joined them on the way. Eventually the group numbered some one hundred and fifty.

Their costumes varied. Some looked vaguely like Mohawk or Narragansett Indians. The men carried axes and hatchets and wore wool blankets and maybe feathers from goose quills. They had smeared their faces with paint, burned cork, charcoal, or soot from the fireplace.

Why Look like Fake Indians?

Besides hiding their identity, there may have been other reasons for the disguises. Many Bostonians feared and respected Mohawk Indians. The rebels may have wanted to appear as fierce as those warriors. Or they might have wanted to look as un-British as possible. Racism may have been at play—the rebels acting and looking like people they considered "savages." We have no record of what real Indians thought of the rebels' unconvincing disguises.

Those who joined along the way had time only
to darken their faces with grease or whatever they

could put their hands on. It was very important
not to be recognized.

A sixteen-year-old boy said later, "We resembled devils from the bottomless pit rather than men."

By the time the "Indians" reached the wharf, a crowd had gathered. As many as one thousand people stayed at the shoreline, in near total silence, to watch what happened next.

Once on the wharf, the "Indians" ran smack into a British officer, who drew his sword. One of the group aimed a gun at him and said, "The  path is wide enough for us all; we have nothing to do with you and intend you no harm—if you keep your own way peaceably, we shall keep ours." The officer wisely stepped aside and let them pass. The men split into three groups and boarded the three ships. They ordered captains and crews belowdecks. Again they promised to do them no harm. Only the chests of tea were in danger. They politely asked for candles and the keys to the hatches. With ropes and pulleys, they hoisted the heavy chests—each weighing four hundred pounds—up onto the decks. They swung their axes—*crackkk!*—to break each chest open. Then they hurled the chests into the ocean.

Chest after chest got dumped in the harbor, all 342 of them, tea leaves flying everywhere.

Carpenters worked side by side with printers, doctors with bricklayers, farmers with barbers— ordinary men all. "I never labored harder in my life," said one man later.

From far away, it might have looked as if the ships were vomiting. It was almost a play performed by the light of torches, lanterns, and the moon.

Those onboard could hear the creaking of the decks, the clomping of men's boots, and the heavy crash of chests hitting water. "Listening from a distance," a British reporter wrote later, "you could hear distinctly the ripping open of the chests and no other sound."

Talking was severely discouraged. The men communicated, when they had to, with whistles or grunts. "We were merry . . . at the idea of making so large a cup of tea for the fishes," a man said later.

They needed to work as fast as possible and then

scram. Punishment for theft in Massachusetts was hanging—a young man had been hanged for it just weeks earlier. This was theft and destruction of property on an unheard-of scale. This was also a crime against England and King George III.

Some forty-six *tons* of tea leaves were seeping into Boston Harbor—an amount worth between $1 and $2 million today.

At any moment, the colonists half expected to be fired at. Indeed, armed British Royal Navy warships were patrolling the harbor that night. Their guns were pointed directly at Griffin's Wharf.

Tea Auctions

Growing and processing tea in China and India took a lot of time and hard work. After the tea leaves were picked, workers filled wooden chests, reportedly stomping on the tea leaves with their bare feet to force as much tea as possible into each chest. Chests were lined with lead to protect the tea on the long sea voyage to London. There, the tea was sold at auction for the highest price. An auctioneer would light a one-inch candle and take bids on chests of tea until the candle went out. The last bidder won the right to buy the tea. The bulk of what went overboard during the Boston Tea Party was bohea. It is an ordinary black tea named for a region near Shanghai, China.

The "Indians" were gambling that the large crowd onshore would protect them, that the British wouldn't risk killing so many innocent bystanders.

The tide was low that night. There was so much tea that some of it accidentally spilled onto the decks of the ships and had to be swept off. Some men stood in the icy, shallow water to chop up the chests so they would sink faster.

The men clearly intended the night to pass

without violence (except toward the tea). They took such care that only one injury was reported. A man was knocked out cold when a chest of tea hit him. His friends carried him onshore to safety and then went right back to work.

Several people tried to steal some of the dumped tea. Not a smart idea. One man was caught stuffing tea into the lining of his coat. He got beaten up.

Another man was seen scooping tea leaves into a canoe. So his canoe got overturned.

Within three hours, it was all over. Men made sure the ship decks were swept clean, and they

shook out their boots over the railing to get rid of any trapped tea. The ships' crews were brought up to check that nothing except the chests had been wrecked.

Then the exhausted boys and men marched back into town.

The harbor was one giant, salty teapot, brimming with what would have made about 18.5 million cups of tea.

What a tea party!

CHAPTER 5
High Spirits—for a Short Time

Everyone got home safely by ten that night. Their coats were fuzzy with tea. Their shoes and boots were still coated with stray tea leaves.

The next day, black leaves blanketed parts of the harbor as far as the eye could see—miles of shoreline. Some of the men went out and beat down the floating tea with oars to prevent it from

being stolen. Some vowed not to eat fish from Boston Harbor for a while because they had been swimming in the hated tea.

One man recalled that they had all "pledged our honor, that we would not reveal our secret." The next day, men probably peeked at each other for telltale signs of soot or paint behind the ears. But the code of secrecy seemed to hold—for years. We *still* don't know all the names of those who took part.

Over fifty years later, a shoemaker named George Hewes broke his silence, saying, "No disorder took place . . . and it was observed at that time that the stillest night ensued that Boston had enjoyed for many months."

The historical record of the event is sketchy. The only pictures we have were done much later on and were not accurate. For example, there were paintings showing a full moon and men in large Indian headdresses. Thousands later claimed to have been present, but their different stories didn't add up.

Historians now say that most "guests" at the Tea Party were young—more than a third were under twenty-one. They came from all walks of life—silversmiths, carpenters, bricklayers, leatherworkers, a butcher, a bookseller, a teacher, a boat builder, merchants, two college graduates.

Paul Revere was probably among them—but not Adams or Hancock. They needed to keep their distance so that they could honestly deny having been present.

Predictably, Governor Hutchinson raged that this was "the boldest stroke that had been struck against British rule in America."

The mood in Boston on December 17 was bubbly. John Adams wrote about "the height of joy that sparkles in the eyes" of everyone on the street. Gleefully he mocked "the disappointed, disconcerted Hutchinson and his tools."

Even Adams, normally prim and proper, called the destruction "magnificent." He wrote, "There is a dignity, a majesty, a sublimity, in this last effort of the Patriots I greatly admire." He was now convinced that the colonies and England could never mend their differences. But at the same time, he was worried. He made a list—called "Bugbears"—of the cruel punishments that

Britain could impose: banning town meetings, overriding local laws, coming up with new taxes, and sending even more troops that Americans would have to house.

The only way to get word of the successful protest to the other colonies was by messenger on horseback. So trusty Paul Revere rode on the only road leading from Boston to New York. It was a

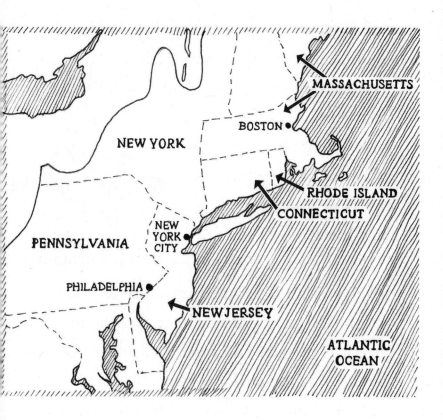

journey of three hundred miles. By December 21 he reached New York, and then he went on to Philadelphia, reaching that city by December 24. From there the news inflamed the colonies.

Did all colonists approve of the Tea Party? No.

Many Southerners, like George Washington, didn't approve of what had happened. Destroying property was criminal. They feared anarchy, or the breakdown of law and order. But many others were inspired by the bold move.

George Washington

News reached England on January 19, 1774, and Parliament swung into action. Destroying the tea was over-the-top, its members felt—an act of war. Parliament charged Samuel Adams and John Hancock—surely they were the ringleaders—with the crime of high treason. If caught, the two were to be brought to England, then hanged. Furthermore, the order said, "while you are still living, your bodies are to be taken down, your bowels torn out . . . your head then cut off, and your bodies divided each into four quarters."

John Hancock ignored the bloody order for his death. He realized now that war with England was certain. He called on people to arm themselves and get ready to "fight for your houses, land, wives, children . . . your liberty and your God" in order that these "vermin will be swept forever from the streets of Boston."

Events would move swiftly after this.

And all of John Adams's "Bugbears"—and more—were to come true.

Today, what happened on the night of December 16 is known as the Boston Tea Party. But back then people referred to the event as "the destruction of the tea" or "the affair." In fact, the phrase "tea parties"—gatherings where women served tea—didn't even come into use until about 1780. The first time the nickname "Boston Tea Party" appeared in print was in 1826, in a newspaper article about a man who "often boasts of the 'Boston tea party.'"

CHAPTER 6
Boston Goes Hungry

Parliament suspected it would be hard to get enough evidence to arrest individuals. So it decided to punish the whole city of Boston. It passed what Americans called the Intolerable Acts. If something is said to be intolerable, it means that people cannot bear it. The idea was to make an example of Boston in order to discourage other cities from rebelling.

Until the city paid for the lost tea, Boston's port was to be shut down. No food could come in, and no goods, either. The only ships allowed in were full of British soldiers. They were there to enforce the law and make sure no more trouble broke out.

Now town meetings were outlawed, and Massachusetts was completely under the king's control.

Even some in Parliament thought that the punishments were too harsh. England was gambling that being so strict would make the city mend its rebel ways. That did not happen.

Soon people were in need of food, but other colonies sent supplies—stores of grain, cattle, sheep from Connecticut, and rice from South Carolina. Samuel Adams was in charge of the committee that handed out food to the neediest.

So the British plan backfired. And Boston's challenge to England inspired other "tea parties" up and down the coast. Mobs, often dressed as Indians, destroyed tea in New York City, Annapolis in Maryland, Greenwich in New Jersey, and Portsmouth in New Hampshire.

John Hancock gloated, "No one circumstance could possibly have taken place more effectually to unite the colonies than this maneuver of the tea."

At an illegal town meeting, Samuel Adams warned, "It is not the rights of Boston only, but of all America which are now struck at. Not the merchants only but the farmer, and every order of men who inhabit this noble continent."

Representatives from Virginia sent this statement: "If our sister colony of Massachusetts Bay is enslaved we cannot long remain free.... UNITED WE STAND, DIVIDED WE FALL."

Thomas Jefferson of Virginia added, "An attack, made on one of our sister colonies . . . is

Thomas Jefferson

an attack made on all British America."

The Tea Party and the Intolerable Acts had sparked unity among the colonists, a feeling that they were all under the thumb of King George. It was time for a meeting of representatives from all the colonies. This had never happened before. It was called the First Continental Congress, an early version of the present-day US Congress.

On September 5, 1774, at Carpenter Hall in Philadelphia, fifty-six representatives met from every colony except Georgia. That was because the people in Georgia still needed the support of British soldiers to protect them against possible Indian attacks.

Every one of the representatives at the Congress was rich or super-rich, except for Samuel Adams. One of them noted Adams's fierceness, saying he "eats little, drinks little, sleeps little, thinks much." The motives of some of the men were selfish. George Washington, one of the richest men in

Carpenter Hall

America, said about the British: "They have no right to put their hands in my pockets." He was talking about his money. He was angry that the British thought that they deserved some of his money and were trying to get it through taxes.

By mid-October the Congress concluded that thirteen of Parliament's actions against the colonies were unjust. They sent a statement to the king demanding certain basic rights such as "life, liberty and property." John Adams was thrilled. He said, "This was one of the happiest days of my life . . . this day convinced me that America will support the [province of] Massachusetts or perish with her."

The representatives all agreed that they had to meet again on May 10, 1775, to discuss the next steps they would take.

Patrick Henry

"I am not a Virginian, but an American."
—Patrick Henry

By November Hancock was calling for twelve thousand men to volunteer as minutemen. (They were known as "minutemen" because they claimed to be ready to fight in sixty seconds.) He had arranged for his last ship sailing from London to be filled with gunpowder. Rebels in Boston stole cannons from the British and named the first two "Hancock" and "Adams."

King George shot back with orders to his troops to crush any revolt. British troops were said to be hunting for Hancock and Adams.

At a large gathering in Virginia in March 1775,

Patrick Henry gave a stunning speech calling for armed rebellion. He announced, "The war is actually begun! . . . I know not what course others may take, but as for me, give me liberty! Or give me death."

King George III: How Mad Was He?

King George III ruled Great Britain for almost sixty years. Though a bit of a tyrant, he was popular (except with the American rebels) and ruled as the mighty British Empire—a "vast empire, on which the sun never sets"—began to flourish. America was its jewel, part of England's plan to rule the world. Certainly he was mad (mad as in angry)

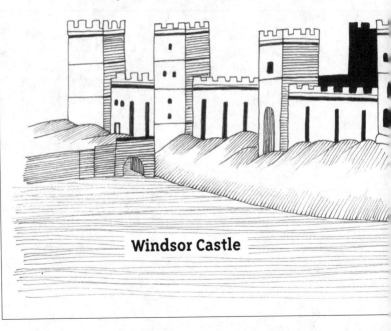

Windsor Castle

at the rebels. His stubbornness in refusing to compromise, backed up by Parliament, led directly to the American Declaration of Independence.

Later in life, George III went insane. His behavior became so strange that he was put into a straitjacket at times. He was known as the Mad King (mad as in mentally ill). Confined to his home in Windsor Castle for the last nine years of his life, he died in 1820.

CHAPTER 7
What the Boston Tea Party Created

By April 18 Paul Revere was taking his famous midnight horseback ride. He was trying to get to Lexington, about eleven miles from Boston. He wanted to warn Hancock and Adams that British troops were coming to capture them. Safely warned, Adams and Hancock could hear gunshots behind them as they escaped.

At the battle of Lexington and Concord, seven hundred British redcoats, the best-trained soldiers in the world, were ambushed by some four thousand American farmers. Someone (we don't know who) fired the first shot of the American Revolutionary War. Men died on both sides, but that day the British were forced to retreat.

"Oh! What a glorious morning is this!"
—Samuel Adams, April 19, 1775, during the
battle of Lexington

As planned, that spring, on May 10, the Second Continental Congress met in Philadelphia. Hancock bought Samuel Adams a complete set of fine new clothes for the meetings. The following month, George Washington, standing head and shoulders above the others, was made commander in chief of the rebel forces. A Southerner, he helped to unite north and south. And Georgia finally joined with the other colonies in the war against England.

The war would last eight painful years. British General Charles Cornwallis surrendered to Washington in 1781, and a peace treaty formally ended the war in 1783.

The thirteen colonies were no longer colonies. They were states now and part of a new country called the United States of America. It was a democracy. There was no king. Laws would be passed by representatives of the citizens.

General Charles Cornwallis

It was the Boston Tea Party that started it all. It led to the American Revolution and the birth of this brand-new, self-governing country.

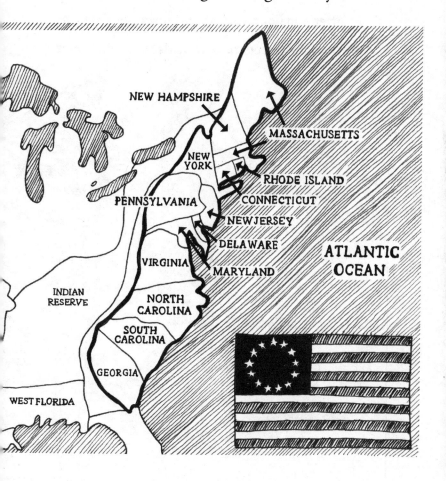

The Surrender at Yorktown

After a major battle at Yorktown, Virginia, the British were forced to accept defeat. What once

had seemed impossible now had happened. The colonists had won the war. At the surrender, the British band played a most fitting song. It was called "The World Turned Upside Down."

CHAPTER 8
After the Party

So much fuss about tea, and yet after the war, coffee became the preferred American drink. It wasn't out of patriotism, but because it was easier to get.

Not everyone in the colonies had wanted to separate from England. Some eighty-five thousand former colonists—many among the more educated and skilled—went to live in Canada, Great Britain,

or the British West Indies. They lost everything they'd built during their lives in the colonies and had to start over again.

Although Ben Franklin was strongly for independence, his son William was against it. He spent almost three years in prison for his loyalty to King George. After that, except for one brief meeting, Ben Franklin never saw his loyalist son again. "Nothing has ever hurt me so much," he mourned. Like many loyalists, William was forced into exile after the war. He lived in England until his death in 1813.

America's victory had ended taxation by the British, but now America had to impose taxes on itself. In fact, taxes soared after the war.

Taxes were needed to pay off the costs of the war, then to set up a new national government and military force.

Because no one died that night, the Tea Party has been the inspiration for nonviolent protests all over the world ever since. In recent years, people have banded together to form a new political group. It is called the Tea Party Movement. They took the name because they see themselves as protesters, too—angry at the high taxes passed by the federal government.

To this day, mystery hovers over the original event. Namely, who were these guys, and what happened to them? Some of their identities leaked out over the years, often after the men had died. We know that some who were teens at the Boston Tea Party became soldiers and officers of the Revolutionary War, and not all survived it.

Those who took part in the Boston Tea Party weren't trying to become famous. They were ordinary people rejecting laws they saw as unjust. They were literally taking matters into their own hands, making their voices heard (without shouting)—and shaping history.

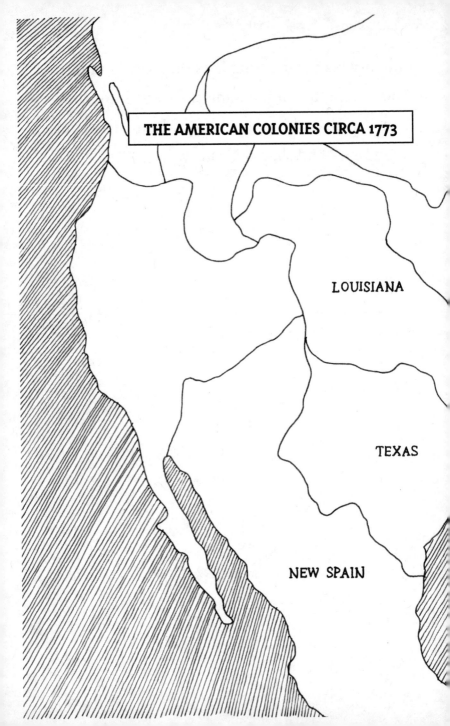

THE AMERICAN COLONIES CIRCA 1773

LOUISIANA

TEXAS

NEW SPAIN

Timeline of the Boston Tea Party

1600	East India Company incorporated
1760	George III ascends to the throne on October 25
1763	The French and Indian War ends
1765	Stamp Act passed, taxing paper documents in the colonies
	Quartering Act passed, requiring colonists to house and feed British soldiers
1767	Townshend Acts passed, taxing tea, glass, paint, and paper in the colonies
1770	Boston Massacre
1773	Tea Act passed, allowing the East India Company to sell tea cheaper and more competitively, but still retaining the tax on tea from the Townshend Acts
1774	Parliament passes a series of laws called the Intolerable Acts by the colonists
1775	The Revolutionary War between the American colonies and Britain begins
1783	The Revolutionary War ends with America's independence
1873	East India Company defunct

Timeline of the World

The first Great Fire of Boston destroys over three hundred buildings	1760
Catherine the Great becomes empress of Russia	1762
Sweden passes the Freedom of the Press Act, becoming the first country to legally protect freedom of the press	1766
Steller's sea cow becomes extinct	1768
Pope Clement XIV succeeds Pope Clement XIII	1769
Fourteen-year-old Marie Antoinette arrives at the French court	1770
Captain James Cook crosses the Antarctic Circle	1773
Louis XVI becomes king of France	1774
The city of San Jose, California, is founded	1777
Astronomer Frederick William Herschel discovers the planet Uranus	1781
The bald eagle becomes the emblem of the United States	1782
Benjamin Franklin invents bifocal glasses	1784
Napoleon becomes a second lieutenant in the French artillery	1785
Delaware ratifies the US Constitution on December 7 and becomes the first state	1787

Bibliography

Books

Alexander, John K. *Samuel Adams: The Life of an American Revolutionary*. Lanham, MD: Rowman & Littlefield, 2011.

*Aronson, Marc. *The Real Revolution: The Global Story of American Independence*. New York: Clarion, 2005.

Earle, Alice Morse. *Home Life in Colonial Days*. Stockbridge, MA: Berkshire House, 1993.

* Fradin, Dennis B. *The Boston Tea Party*. New York: Benchmark Books, 2007.

*———. *Samuel Adams: The Father of American Independence*. New York: Clarion, 1998.

* Gondosch, Linda. *How Did Tea and Taxes Spark a Revolution?: And Other Questions about the Boston Tea Party*. Minneapolis, MN: Lerner, 2010.

Griswold, Wesley S. *The Night the Revolution Began: The Boston Tea Party, 1773*. Brattleboro, VT: Stephen Greene Press, 1972.

* Kroll, Steven. *The Boston Tea Party*. New York: Holiday House, 1998.

Labaree, Benjamin Woods. *The Boston Tea Party*. New York: Oxford University Press, 1964.

Langguth, A. J. *Patriots: The Men Who Started the American Revolution*. New York: Simon & Schuster, 1988.

Lepore, Jill. *The Whites of Their Eyes: The Tea Party's Revolution and the Battle over American History*. Princeton, NJ: Princeton University Press, 2010.

Marten, James, ed. *Children in Colonial America*. New York: New York University Press, 2007.

Stoll, Ira. *Samuel Adams: A Life*. New York: Free Press, 2008.

Unger, Harlow Giles. *American Tempest: How the Boston Tea Party Sparked a Revolution*. Cambridge, MA: Da Capo Press, 2011.

*Books for young readers

Bibliography

Websites

Boston 1775. Blog by J. L. Bell.
   http://boston1775.blogspot.com/.
Boston Massacre Historical Society.
   http://bostonmassacre.net/.
The Boston Tea Party (lesson plans). National
   Endowment for the Humanities.
   http://edsitement. neh.gov/lesson-plan/boston-
   tea-party-costume-optional/.
Boston Tea Party Historical Society.
   http://boston-tea-party.org/
Boston Tea Party Ships and Museum.
   http://www.bostonteapartyship.com/.
The Freedom Trail.
   http://www.oldsouthmeetinghouse.org/.
Tax History Museum.
   http://www.taxhistory.org/www/website.nsf/Web/
   TaxHistoryMuseum? OpenDocument/.